Sky High

THE TRUE STORY OF MAGGIE GEE

BY **MARISSA MOSS**

ILLUSTRATED BY **CARL ANGEL**

TRICYCLE PRESS
Berkeley | Toronto

WHEN I WAS LITTLE, something special happened every Sunday. Other families went to baseball games or the movies, but not mine. Instead we would drive out to the airport. We weren't going on a trip or meeting someone from a flight. We went to watch the airplanes. For us, nothing could be as exciting as watching the planes take off. We loved how they bumped clumsily along the runway, only to suddenly leap up, break free from the ground, and soar away, far away, until the black speck of the plane disappeared. My brothers, sisters, and I would lick our only-on-Sunday lollipops and tip our heads back, letting the roar of the engines fill our ears. I loved how the vibrations echoed in my bones. Just being there, being part of it all, made me feel big and powerful.

I liked to search for my favorite pilot, Amelia Earhart. She had flown all the way across the ocean by herself, and I wanted to be just like her. Once I'm sure I saw her. When I waved, she saw me and waved back. It had to be her—I didn't know of any other women pilots back then. Just Amelia Earhart. And me. Well, I would be a pilot someday.

I told my brothers and sisters stories of how I would fly across the oceans, over deserts, and around the world. I described flying around the Eiffel Tower, tracing the line of the Great Wall of China from the air, looping over the pyramids.

"Will you take me with you?" Lucy, my youngest sister, begged.

"No, me!" demanded my brother, James.

"I'll take all of you," I said, "if you pay me with one Sunday lollipop." It was a high price, I knew. But flying in an airplane—that would be worth it. When my mother heard my offer, she laughed.

"Save your lollipops," she said. "Maggie is just telling you stories. Some stories are true, and some are made up. Now, I tell true stories."

And then she would tell us about life in China, where she and my father had lived before they came to America. She talked about fetching water from a well when it was so cold that the ice had to be broken before she could dip in her bucket. She talked about festivals when the whole village danced in the streets in bright, silk clothing, and tables were set up outside for everyone to eat together.

Her stories felt as far away as China, and nothing like our life in California. They were like dreams—beautiful and mysterious, impossible to touch. *My stories are truer than that,* I thought. One day, I would be able to taste and smell and feel my stories. One day, I would make them come true.

When Grandmother heard my stories, she said, "I tell stories that are already true, not yet-to-be true." Sometimes she would tell us about China, like my mother did, but mostly she told stories about the farm she and Grandfather had here. She told of bad-luck weather and shriveled crops and good-luck weather and rich harvests. She told of plums as big as her fist and hail as big as our toes. These stories felt real to me, but they weren't mine.

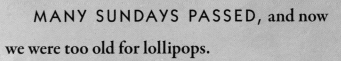

MANY SUNDAYS PASSED, and now
we were too old for lollipops.

I didn't tell stories anymore, but I still dreamed of flying.

Until a nightmare happened—a war, a very big war. So big, the whole world was fighting, and it was called World War II. Everyone did what they could to help. My brothers joined the army, and my mother worked as a welder building Liberty ships to transport troops.

"You can work here with me," she said. "Do some good for your country."

"I will work for my country," I agreed, "but in my own way. Now is my chance to fly."

I had read about a group of women pilots called the WASP, or Women Airforce Service Pilots. They flew planes on training missions and ferried bombers to military airbases. I knew right away that I wanted to join them. I would be doing something important for the war, and I would be able to fly. If I could only earn my wings. . . .

First, I had to go to flight school to learn how to fly a plane. That summer, two girlfriends and I bought a car together. It didn't matter that none of us knew how to use it yet. I taught myself to drive on the long trip to flight school.

The first time I got to fly alone—to "solo"—was just as I had imagined. The earth rolled beneath me, green and yellow and brown, and I was free in the clouds. As fields and barns rushed by under me, I thought of Grandmother's stories of her farm. My grandparents had worked such land. Now here I was high above, plowing the air.

I was a good pilot, good enough to be chosen to go on for training as a WASP. The girlfriends who had driven out with me weren't picked, but at least now they knew how to drive and could get themselves home. I stayed behind, eager to be up in the air as much as possible.

WASP training was much tougher than flight school. We did the same intense work the male pilots had to do. I learned to parachute and make emergency landings. I learned to loop the loop, and fly low over cows' heads, surprising them. It was hard and tiring and wonderful, all at once.

The day that I earned my wings and was made a WASP,
I was so proud that I felt as if I could fly without an airplane.
I sent my mother a postcard. All I wrote was: "Some stories
are true, some are not. This is a true story." My family's stories
flew with me, but now I was living out my own true stories.

Some missions were fun, like flying in formation with other WASP, waiting for the male fighter pilots to attack us. They were also in training and didn't attack our planes, just the banners behind us. But they used live ammunition, even for practice. For me, it was like playing tag in the air.

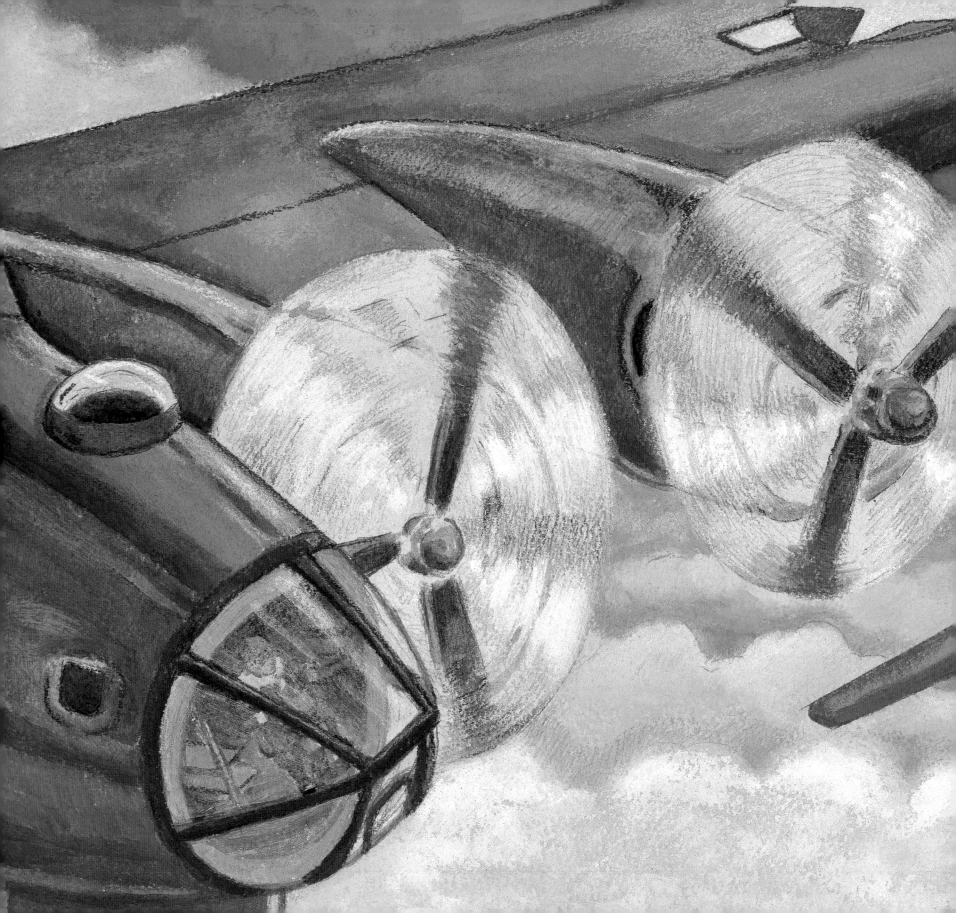

Other missions were scary. Once I had to fly across the country late in the day. As the sun slipped lower and lower, and the sky grew darker and darker, I couldn't see to fly. I needed to land, but bigger planes churned the air next to me with their giant propellers and my small plane almost tipped over.

I landed all right, but I did bump into another plane on the runway. The other pilot and I both stepped out on shaky legs to see if the planes were okay. When the pilot saw me, he tensed up and stared hard. There were plenty of other WASP, so I knew that he wasn't surprised to see a woman climb from the cockpit, but he must have been startled to see an Asian face. I could tell that he was mistaking me for an enemy pilot, a Japanese kamikaze, or a spy. I had heard it all before, but this time I didn't get angry. Instead, I smiled and said a big hello.

"You're American?" he asked nervously.

"Born and bred," I answered and offered my hand to shake.

"Well, don't that beat all," he said. "Never thought I'd see the day."

I felt like an exhibit at the county fair, a two-headed cow, the amazing Chinese American WASP. But only for a minute. I got back in my plane and once more was a pilot, plain and simple. I felt big and strong again, and no one could take that feeling away.

The days passed with me soaring high in the heavens, looping the loop and rolling for fun, but working hard, too. I was helping my country to win the war, but I was also helping myself— making my own stories and dreams come true.

Now I tell these stories to my children and grandchildren, and my tales must seem as far away to them as China. They cannot imagine such a war. They cannot imagine being one of only two Chinese American pilots in the WASP. They cannot imagine trying to fly at night with only your eyes to guide you.

But my stories aren't yet-to-be-true anymore because I earned my wings. Now they're already-true.

Author's Note

This book is based on the life of Maggie Gee, who, growing up during the 1930s in the San Francisco Bay Area, watched the planes take off and land at the Oakland airport, hoping for a glimpse of Amelia Earhart. When the United States entered World War II (WWII) in 1941, Maggie was a freshman at the University of California at Berkeley. To contribute to the war effort, she quit school and worked as a draftsperson for the military, but that wasn't enough for Maggie. She and two friends decided to go to flight school with the hopes of joining the Women Airforce Service Pilots (WASP) and fighting for their country. They pooled their money, bought a car for $25, and headed for Texas, where the WASP trained.

When the U.S. Air Force started recruiting female pilots, more than 25,000 women applied. Only 1,830 were accepted into flight school; of these, 1,037 graduated. The women who earned their wings proved themselves to be strong, competent pilots and worked hard in similar conditions as men did. Though not allowed in combat, they flew a combined sixty million miles of missions, and 38 of these pilots died in the line of duty.

When Maggie graduated from the tough course of training, she was one of only two Chinese Americans in the WASP. She was stationed in Las Vegas, Nevada, where she helped train other pilots—both male and female. While the government needed the extra fighters at the height of the war, it disbanded the WASP in 1944, after just two years, shortly before the end of WWII. It would be another thirty years before women were allowed in the cockpit of a U.S. military plane again.

Maggie went back to school and made more of her dreams come true. She joined the army in the 1950s, running service clubs in Germany during the height of the Cold War. Later she became a physicist, working for the Lawrence Livermore Laboratory until she retired. Today, Maggie is active in local politics and continues to meet regularly with her WASP friends. Of the original thousand who earned their wings, only a couple hundred are still alive, but their story lives on.

For more information about the Women Airforce Service Pilots, visit www.wingsacrossamerica.us

1: Maggie's grandmother, Jung So Young, in formal dress, China, c.1900.

2: Maggie's mother, Marion Gee, building Liberty ships at the Kaiser Richmond Shipyards, Richmond, CA, 1945.

3: Maggie in front of an A-6 Army Air Force trainer, Avenger Field, Sweetwater, TX, 1944.

4: Maggie (back row, right) with three of her siblings, Berkeley, CA, 1930.

5: Maggie in flight uniform, 1944.

6: Maggie in full flight uniform at the WWII pilots' reunion, Moffett Field, CA, 2008.

BACK COVER: Maggie in the cockpit of a Stearman biplane, Avenger Field, Sweetwater, TX, 1944.

For Rob, who dreams of flying high.
—MM

For my son, Jun, my wife, Holly,
and to Dan and Loretta San Souci
for bringing us together.
—CA

Acknowledgments

I want to thank Maggie Gee for generously sharing her story and for inspiring generations after her to break boundaries and follow their dreams.
—MM

I would like to thank the following people for their help in the illustration reference process of this book: Angela, Kelsey, Emma, and Hunter Angel-Baehrens; Janine Macbeth; Pamela Kruse-Buckingham and Richard Hume of the Oakland Aerospace Museum; Ann Yee; Holly Kim; Abe Ignacio; Christine Araneta; and Vicki Wong.
—CA

On behalf of the author and illustrator, the publisher would like to thank Nancy Parrish of Wings Across America for her expert and careful review of this book.

Tricycle Press
an imprint of Ten Speed Press
PO Box 7123
Berkeley, California 94707
www.tricyclepress.com

Design by Katy Brown
Typeset in Garamond, Kabel, and Sign Painter
The illustrations in this book were rendered in acrylics and colored pencil.

Library of Congress Cataloging-in-Publication Data

Moss, Marissa.
    Sky high : the true story of Maggie Gee / by Marissa Moss ; illustrated by Carl Angel.
      p. cm.
    ISBN-13: 978-1-58246-280-6 (hardcover)
    ISBN-10: 1-58246-280-1 (hardcover)
    1. Gee, Maggie. 2. World War, 1939-1945—Aerial operations, American—Juvenile literature. 3. Women Airforce Service Pilots (U.S.)—Biography—Juvenile literature. 4. World War, 1939-1945—Participation, Female—Juvenile literatur. 5. Women air pilots—United States—Biography—Juvenile literature. 6. Air pilots, Military—United States—Biography—Juvenile literature. I. Angel, Carl. II. Title.
    D790.5.M67 2009
    940.54'4973092—dc22
    [B]
                                    2008042387

First Tricycle Press printing, 2009
Printed in China

1 2 3 4 5 6 — 13 12 11 10 09